James H. Fassett

illustrated by
Ernest Shepard

Ginn

As a graded anthology of traditional tales, myths and legends from all over the world the Beacon Readers have never been equalled. They have been loved by generations of children and valued by their teachers since the 1920s. In this latest edition the original volume has been divided into two for greater flexibility and to make it more inviting to the reader. The opportunity has also been taken to alter the occasional awkward turn of phrase resulting from the constraints of the Beacon phonic system and the age of the original text.

The Pancake follows *Old Dog Tom* and *Little Chick Chick* in the Beacon grading sequence.

The stories' naturally rhythmic and repetitive style and their charm and appeal, enhanced by Ernest Shepard's classic illustrations, encourage fluent reading and the formation of the reading habit.

In the Beacon Library at this level are: *The Wise Little Goat* (ISBN 0 602 20161 6), *The Dragon Princess* (ISBN 0 602 20148 9) and *The Golden Fish* (ISBN 0 602 20152 7).

© James H. Fassett 1922
Revised edition 1931
Second revised edition 1957
Third revised edition 1981
Seventy-fifth impression 1994 01-759407
The Pancake 2 book set ISBN 0 602 22508 6

Published by Ginn and Company Ltd
Prebendal House, Parson's Fee
Aylesbury, Bucks HP20 2QZ

Printed in Hong Kong by Bookbuilders Ltd

Contents

The Pancake *Norse Folk Tale*	4
The Old Woman and Her Pig *English Folk Tale*	12
The House that Jack Built *Nursery Rhyme*	24
In Bed	33
Chicken Licken *English Folk Tale*	34

The Pancake

A big fat cook made a big fat pancake.

Near the cook were seven hungry little boys.

"We like big round pancakes, Mr. Cook," said all the little boys.

"This pancake will be good to eat," said Mr. Cook.

But the pancake in the pan said,

"I will not, not, not be eaten."

So the big round pancake gave a hop.

The pancake gave a jump.

And off he rolled out of the pan.

Mr. Pancake rolled round and round and round.

And oh! so very, very fast.

"Stop! Stop! Mr. Pancake!" said the cook.

But the pancake rolled faster and faster.

Then the big fat cook began to run after the pancake.

"Stop! Stop!" said all the little boys.

But the pancake rolled faster and faster.

Then all the little boys began to run.

The pancake met a little man.

"Stop, Pancake, stop! I am hungry! I want to eat you," said the little man.

"The cook can't stop me.

The boys can't stop me.

You can't stop me," said the pancake, and rolled faster and faster.

Then the little man began to run.

The pancake met a hen.

"Stop, Pancake, stop! I am very hungry!

I want to eat you," said the hen.

"The cook can't stop me.

The boys can't stop me.

The man can't stop me.

You can't stop me."

And the pancake rolled faster than ever.

Then the hen began to run.

The pancake met a duck.

"Stop, Pancake, stop! I am very, very hungry!

I want to eat you," said the duck.

"The cook can't stop me.

The boys can't stop me.

The man can't stop me.

The hen can't stop me.

You can't stop me."

And the pancake rolled faster and faster.

The pancake met a pig.

"Why do you run so fast?" said the pig.

"Can't you see?

The cook, the boys, the man, the hen, and the duck all want to eat me."

"That is too bad. I will run with you," said the pig.

So the pig and the pancake went on and on and on.

They came to a wide pond.

"I can't swim," said the pancake.

"I can," said the pig.

"Jump upon my nose, and I will take you across."

So the pancake jumped upon the pig's nose.

The pig gave a big grunt.

And snip! snap! he ate up the big round pancake.

Yes, the pig ate up every bit.

The Old Woman and Her Pig

One day an old woman found a penny.

"What can I do with this penny?" said she.

"I will go to the market and buy a pig."

So the old woman bought a pig.

Then she tied a string to the pig's leg.

On her way home she came to a stile.

The pig would not go over the stile.

She went a little farther and met a dog.

She said to the dog,

"Dog, dog, bite pig;

Pig won't go over stile,
And I shan't get home to-night."
But the dog would not.
She went a little farther and met a stick.

"Stick, stick, beat dog;
Dog won't bite pig,
Pig won't go over stile,
And I shan't get home to-night."

But the stick would not.

She went a little farther and met a fire.

"Fire, fire, burn stick;
Stick won't beat dog,
Dog won't bite pig,
Pig won't go over stile,
And I shan't get home to-night."
But the fire would not.

She went a little farther and met some water.

"Water, water, put out fire;
Fire won't burn stick,
Stick won't beat dog,
Dog won't bite pig,
Pig won't go over stile,
And I shan't get home to-night."
But the water would not.

She went a little farther and met an ox.

"Ox, ox, drink water;
Water won't put out fire,
Fire won't burn stick,
Stick won't beat dog,
Dog won't bite pig,
Pig won't go over stile,
And I shan't get home to-night."
But the ox would not.

She went a little farther and met a man.

"Man, man, kill ox;
Ox won't drink water,
Water won't put out fire,
Fire won't burn stick,
Stick won't beat dog,
Dog won't bite pig,
Pig won't go over stile,
And I shan't get home to-night."
But the man would not.

She went a little farther and met a rope.

"Rope, rope, hang man;
Man won't kill ox,
Ox won't drink water,
Water won't put out fire,
Fire won't burn stick,
Stick won't beat dog,
Dog won't bite pig,
Pig won't go over stile,
And I shan't get home to-night."
But the rope would not.

She went a little farther and met a rat.

"Rat, rat, bite rope;
Rope won't hang man,
Man won't kill ox,
Ox won't drink water,
Water won't put out fire,
Fire won't burn stick,
Stick won't beat dog,
Dog won't bite pig,
Pig won't go over stile,
And I shan't get home to-night."
But the rat would not.

She went a little farther and met a cat.

"Cat, cat, kill rat;
Rat won't bite rope,
Rope won't hang man,
Man won't kill ox,
Ox won't drink water,
Water won't put out fire,
Fire won't burn stick,
Stick won't beat dog,
Dog won't bite pig,
Pig won't go over stile,
And I shan't get home to-night."

The cat said, "You must get me some milk.

Then I will kill the rat."

So the old woman went to the cow and said,

"Cow, cow, will you give me some milk?"

The cow said, "Get me a pail of water to drink.

Then I will give you some milk."

So the old woman took a pail of water to the cow.

And the cow gave her some milk.

Then the old woman gave the milk to the cat.

The cat began to kill the rat,
The rat began to bite the rope,
The rope began to hang the man,
The man began to kill the ox,
The ox began to drink the water,
The water began to put out the fire,
The fire began to burn the stick,
The stick began to beat the dog,
The dog began to bite the pig,
And the pig jumped over the stile.

So the old woman got home with her pig that night.

The House that Jack Built

This is the house that Jack built.

This is the malt,
That lay in the house that Jack built.

This is the rat,
That ate the malt,
That lay in the house that Jack built.

This is the cat,
That killed the rat,
That ate the malt,
That lay in the house that Jack built.

This is the dog,
That worried the cat,
That killed the rat,
That ate the malt,
That lay in the house that Jack built.

This is the cow with the crumpled horn,
That tossed the dog,
That worried the cat,
That killed the rat,
That ate the malt,
That lay in the house that Jack built.

This is the maiden all forlorn,
That milked the cow with the crumpled horn,
That tossed the dog,
That worried the cat,
That killed the rat,
That ate the malt,
That lay in the house that Jack built.

This is the man all tattered and torn,
That kissed the maiden all forlorn,
That milked the cow with the crumpled horn,
That tossed the dog,
That worried the cat,
That killed the rat,
That ate the malt,
That lay in the house that Jack built.

This is the priest all shaven and shorn,
That married the man all tattered and torn,
That kissed the maiden all forlorn,
That milked the cow with the crumpled horn,
That tossed the dog,
That worried the cat,
That killed the rat,
That ate the malt,
That lay in the house that Jack built.

This is the cock that crowed in the morn,
That woke the priest all shaven and shorn,
That married the man all tattered and torn,
That kissed the maiden all forlorn,
That milked the cow with the crumpled horn,
That tossed the dog,
That worried the cat,
That killed the rat,
That ate the malt,
That lay in the house that Jack built.

This is the farmer sowing his corn,
That kept the cock that crowed in the morn,
That woke the priest all shaven and shorn,
That married the man all tattered and torn,
That kissed the maiden all forlorn,
That milked the cow with the crumpled horn,
That tossed the dog,
That worried the cat,
That killed the rat,
That ate the malt,
That lay in the house that Jack built.

In Bed

"I see the moon,
    and the moon sees me.
God bless the moon,
    and God bless me."

Chicken Licken

Chicken Licken went to the woods one day.

An acorn fell upon her little head.

She thought the sky had fallen.

She said, "I will go and tell the king.

I will tell the king that the sky has fallen."

So Chicken Licken turned back and met Hen Len.

"Well, Hen Len, where are you going?"

And Hen Len said,

"I am going to the woods for some food."

Chicken Licken said, "Oh, Hen Len, don't go.

I was going, and the sky fell upon my poor little head.

Now I am going to tell the king."

So Hen Len turned back with Chicken Licken.

They met Cock Lock.

"Well, Cock Lock, where are you going?"

And Cock Lock said, "I am going to the woods for some food."

Hen Len said, "Oh, Cock Lock, don't go.

I was going, and I met Chicken Licken.

Chicken Licken was going to the woods.

There the sky fell upon her poor little head.

Now we are going to tell the king."

So Cock Lock turned back and met Duck Luck.

"Well, Duck Luck, where are you going?"

Duck Luck said, "I am going to the woods for some food."

Cock Lock said, "Oh, Duck Luck, don't go.

I was going, and I met Hen Len.

Hen Len met Chicken Licken.

Chicken Licken was going to the woods.

There the sky fell upon her poor little head.

Now we are going to tell the king."

So Duck Luck turned back and met Drake Lake.

"Well, Drake Lake, where are you going?"

Drake Lake said, "I am going to the woods for some food."

Duck Luck said, "Oh, Drake Lake, don't go.

I was going, and I met Cock Lock.
Cock Lock met Hen Len.
Hen Len met Chicken Licken.
Chicken Licken was going to the woods.
There the sky fell upon her poor little head.
Now we are going to tell the king."

So Drake Lake turned back and met Goose Loose.

"Well, Goose Loose, where are you going?"

Goose Loose said, "I am going to the woods for some food."

Drake Lake said, "Oh, Goose Loose, don't go.

I was going, and I met Duck Luck.

Duck Luck met Cock Lock.

Cock Lock met Hen Len.

Hen Len met Chicken Licken.

Chicken Licken was going to the woods.

There the sky fell upon her poor little head.

Now we are going to tell the king."

So Goose Loose turned back and met Gander Lander.

"Well, Gander Lander, where are you going?"

Gander Lander said, "I am going to the woods for some food."

Goose Loose said, "Oh, Gander Lander, don't go.

I was going, and I met Drake Lake.
Drake Lake met Duck Luck.
Duck Luck met Cock Lock.
Cock Lock met Hen Len.
Hen Len met Chicken Licken.

Chicken Licken was going to the woods.

There the sky fell upon her poor little head.

Now we are going to tell the king."

So Gander Lander turned back and met Turkey Lurkey.

"Well, Turkey Lurkey, where are you going?"

Turkey Lurkey said, "I am going to the woods for some food."

Gander Lander said, "Oh, Turkey Lurkey, don't go.

I was going, and I met Goose Loose.

Goose Loose met Drake Lake.

Drake Lake met Duck Luck.

Duck Luck met Cock Lock.

Cock Lock met Hen Len.

Hen Len met Chicken Licken.

Chicken Licken was going to the woods.

There the sky fell upon her poor little head.

Now we are going to tell the king."

So Turkey Lurkey turned back.
He walked with Gander Lander.
Goose Loose walked with Drake Lake.
Duck Luck walked with Cock Lock.
Hen Len walked with Chicken Licken.

As they were going along they met Fox Lox.

Fox Lox said, "Where are you all going?"

They said, "Chicken Licken was going to the woods.

The sky fell upon her poor little head.

Now we are going to tell the king."

Fox Lox said, "Come with me. I will show you the way to the king."

But Fox Lox took them into his den.

He and his little foxes soon ate up poor Chicken Licken, Hen Len, Cock Lock, Duck Luck, Drake Lake, Goose Loose, Gander Lander, and Turkey Lurkey.

So they never saw the king.

And they never told him that the sky had fallen.